Bangladesh at Work

BANGLADESH
at work

Caroline Feller Bauer

ℒℒ The University Press Limited

The University Press Limited
Red Crescent House
61 Motijheel Commercial Area
G.P.O. Box 2611
Dhaka 1000
Bangladesh

Fax: (88 02) 9565443
E-mail: upl@bangla.net, upl@bttb.net.bd
Website: www.uplbooks.com

First Published, 2006

Credits
Text and photographs: Caroline Feller Bauer
Book layout and cover design: Ashraful Hassan Arif

Front cover: Dhaka Duck
Back cover: Brick Breaking
End paper: Factory scene at Youngone Group, CEPZ

ISBN 984 05 1765 1

Published by Mohiuddin Ahmed, The University Press Limited, Dhaka. This book has been set in GillSans by Color Horizon and produced by Abarton, Malibagh, Dhaka. Printed at the Akota Offset Press, 119 Fakirapool, Dhaka, Bangladesh.

Introduction

As 'progress' comes to Bangladesh, most of the handwork and street vendors shown in this book will be only a memory, so:

Bangladeshis: this book is for you to keep on your shelves to share with your grandchildren.

Foreign Business Travelers: You may only get a glimpse of 'Bangladesh at work' as you navigate the traffic on the way to your hotel, factory, or airport. Here is a readymade souvenir of this intriguing country.

Tourists: These photos are for you to take home, so you can show your family and friends the real Bangladesh.

And, this book is for anyone who loves Bangladesh and wants to enjoy the country from his or her own living room.

It has been a delight to live in such an interesting country as Bangladesh. Although, of course, it has its share of doctors, lawyers, and other professional workers, it is the small village vendors and workers that have intrigued me. I have tried to capture, in photos, the traditional work that is disappearing as fast as mobile phones and computers begin to invade the landscape. Living in Bangladesh is like living in a history book since the way it is, is the way it was.

My Bangladesh

'I wouldn't go live there if you gave me ten million dollars,' said the waiter at the Fontainebleau Buffet, in Miami Beach when I told him that we were about to move to Bangladesh.

On my first trip back home, I raced back to the same restaurant to tell the waiter how much we loved Bangladesh. Alas, he no longer worked there.

Maybe he will see this book, and discover what a unique and fascinating country this is and come to visit it some day!

What do I like about Bangladesh?

I begin with the people. They are just plain super nice: Hospitable, accepting, curious, hard working, oh, and good looking.

The climate? The Bangladeshi winter is the best kept secret of the tourist industry. Winter is a particular delight with cloudless days and spring temperatures. A British gardening friend arrived here in the summer and was disappointed that she couldn't make a garden grow. And then, the glorious winter arrived with its bright colorful flowers. And the summer? Yes. It rains, but the monsoon months are so interesting with the dynamic rain, and the luscious green of the foliage and rice fields. OK, it can be hot, but some of us (me) like the heat.

The most intriguing part of Bangladesh is the fact that so far it hasn't 'developed' so that it doesn't look like every other place on the planet. However, that's coming in the future. Shopping malls are beginning to replace the small open shops. Supermarkets are replacing the open markets. Machines are replacing bullock power in the fields and in the brickyards.

Some village housewives are now cooking on gas stoves rather than handmade clay stoves. The popular cycle rickshaws and street vendors pushing cycle-vans are being moved away to control the traffic flow and some day they will disappear from the streets.

Industries are also changing. They are becoming more hightech. Walk into a condensed milk factory and all you see are machines: no cows, no milk.

One of the cottage industries is salt processing. These salt sheds seem quite primitive, but they employ many workers. Now, a foreign business consultant has arrived in Bangladesh to supervise the building of a modern salt plant. These changes are probably inevitable if Bangladesh wants to compete in the world market, but it is a pity to see the old ways go.

Presently, Bangladesh feels like an intimate family living in a history book village. In fact, it sometimes seems as though everyone is related to everyone else. It truly is one big family!

Here, in Bangladesh a shopper can buy one cigarette, an envelope or a pencil from a small shop. In America, you are compelled to buy a package of two dozen pencils from a huge office store.

In Bangladesh you can still buy fresh food, even freshly rolled spices from the numerous 'hotels' in the cities and in the villages.

Bangladesh is the ultimate recycling country. Old newspapers are made into paper bags, and old ships become building materials for new construction.

This book is meant to celebrate the workers of Bangladesh.

They have my respect and admiration.

Thank you for letting me take your photo.

Caroline Bauer

Chittagong, Bangladesh

Forge

At this shop, you can buy a knife, forged by the artisan.

Typist

If you need your letter to look professional, or don't know how to write, these typists near the courthouse or stock exchange will help you.

This man will help you fill in your visa form, for a fee, on the street, outside a foreign consulate.

Form Filler

What a unique service this man performs!

Ear Cleaner

Mood Rings

If you need a good luck charm, you can buy a ring to grant your wish for good health or a successful business venture.

Hauling

An amazing variety of goods are transported by vehicles plying the roads of Bangladesh. You can hire the handcart whenever you need to haul commercial or personal property.

Drivers are adept at piling almost anything onto their rickshaws. Tempos are private buses carrying people and their wares inside and outside the vehicle.

Water Carriers

Many people do not have access to clean water. Women and children fetch the water in aluminum pots. You can also buy water from a vendor or pay someone to bring it to you.

Markets

Vendors sell fruit and vegetables in open markets. Betel nuts and leaves are prepared for paan chewers.

Rice

Rice, a major crop of Bangladesh, is usually grown in small fields as a family business. Seeing the whole process from planting to harvest gives you the feeling of the changing seasons.

Street Repairs

A cobbler, an umbrella maker and a saw sharpener offer their services on the street.

Tailor

Although Bangladesh is one of the poorest countries in the world, some traditions seem 'rich' to Westerners. Many people have their clothes made to order. Women have their salwar kameezes stitched at the tailor shop and men have their shirts and pants made to measure. City girls sport the salwar kameez while enjoying ice cream cones.

Sari Salesman

The traditional dress for women is the sari—six yards of fabric draped around the body. These are village girls dressed for the Hindu festival of Durga Puja.

Ship Breaking

Ever wonder where old ships go to die? Chittagong is a destination for old tankers and cruise ships that are no longer profitable to sail.

The old ships are run up onto the beach at full moon (when the tide is highest). Workers then tear apart the whole ship. The entire steel hull, furniture, engines, books, life jackets — virtually everything is salvaged and sold.

Ship Breaking Goods

Toilets and stainless steel sinks are typical of the items for sale from the Bangladesh ship breaking industry.

Bird Hawker

Don't ask where the birds are caught. And, don't trust the bright colors. One shower and the colors will disappear! Still, you can buy a treasured pet from this hawker.

Fortune Tellers

*Offer a few takas to the fortune teller and the bird will choose
an envelope containing your fortune.*

Hold the hand of the monkey and the fortune teller will tell you your future.

Laundry

Women wash their pots and clothes in the village pond. A commercial laundry dries shirts along the street.

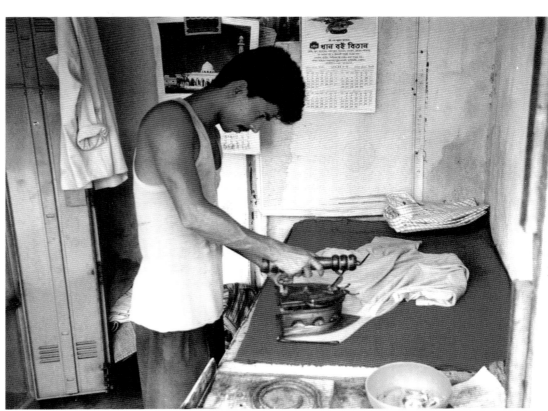

Presser

Years ago I bought an antique clothes iron heated by coal. Imagine my surprise when I saw the same type of iron in use in Bangladesh. Although there is electricity in this village, it is cheaper to use a coal iron to keep costs down.

Salt Production

Raw salt is brought from the beaches by barges. The process is simple: clean and boil the salt, add iodine and package. Here, it is sold directly to the customer from a pushcart.

Iceman

*Ice is transported from the ice plant and
used by produce and fish vendors.*

Butcher

Cows are slaughtered early in the morning. The beef is for sale at neighborhood outdoor shops or offered in portions on city streets or village fields.

Brick Making

Bricks are essential for building since wood is expensive and there are not enough stones in Bangladesh. Brick makers are paid by how many bricks they produce. Dried first in the sun, bricks are baked in large underground pits fueled by charcoal.

Brick Breaker

Brick 'seconds' are hammered into small pieces to be used to make concrete for road and building construction. The old and young engaged in this work are paid by how many bricks they break.

Fishmonger

Fresh and dried fish are staples in the Bangladesh diet.

Pole Fisherman

A fisherman sets up his perch in the middle of the river and casts his net from above.

Embroiderer

Many small boutiques employ their own embroiderers, block printers and tailors.

Scrap Sorters

A mountain of fabric scraps, discarded by garment factories, is sorted by type of fiber.

Cotton, polyester and nylon are recycled into paper or stuffing for cushions and mattresses.

Coconut Fiber Rope Maker

Bangladesh is the recycle capital of the world. Here, workers have scraped the fiber from discarded coconut shells and are making rope. Coconut fibers are also used as stuffing for mattresses and cushions.

The Classic

Collecting photos of Bangladesh?
This is a must because it is the 'Wow!' of handcart pullers.

Tea Taster

Tea Picker

Tea is big business in Bangladesh. Women are the pickers. How can you tell if a new crop of tea is worth buying? Taste it. The tea is brewed and tested for taste, color, strength and aroma.

Fuel Sticks

Cow manure is a cheap fuel and can also be a source of income.
The manure is molded over wooden sticks, dried in the sun and fed
into the hole on the side of a clay stove.

House Performers

Elephants and snake charmers perform in front of private homes.

Dhaka Duck

How do you get your purchases home? Let him (or is it her?) ride as a passenger.

Fishnet Repair

*This is a never-ending chore: making and repairing fishnets.
The men work together or by themselves. The rope is held
between the toes to give the workmen another 'hand.'*

Tupi Salesman

The small skullcap or *tupi* is sold in the markets or on the street and worn while praying. The first of five daily prayer times is held at first light. It is not uncommon to go back to sleep or catch a short nap before the working day begins.

Rag Pickers

Small children search the gutters for anything that can be sold or recycled. The election posters are being stripped from the wall just two minutes after the polls open. The paper will probably be used to make shopping bags.

The rag pickers stop their work to catch a glimpse of a black and white TV program from the back wall of a cafe.

School Bus Driver

I would have loved to have gone to school in a rickshaw school bus.
These are popular throughout Bangladesh.

Painters

Using a bamboo platform, these painters are putting a coat of paint on a new building.
The humid weather keeps painters busy painting old buildings too.

Sign Painter

Announcing a mobile phone service is just one of the jobs for a sign painter. Banners are painted for meetings and celebrations.

Rug Painter

Colored jute is used to weave designs in machine-made or hand-made jute rugs. When the design fades, the rug is simply repainted by hand.

Wedding Kitchen

The kitchens at the wedding halls feed hundreds and even thousands of guests. Everything is freshly prepared. Chickens and cows are slaughtered on site. The cooks' helpers prepare spices and cut up vegetables.

Medicine Men

Itinerant medicine men turn up at different locations everyday. You can have your 'bad blood' sucked by a leech or a hollowed-out buffalo horn for a small fee.

The 'dentist' sets up his tools and sample dentures at a small marketplace.

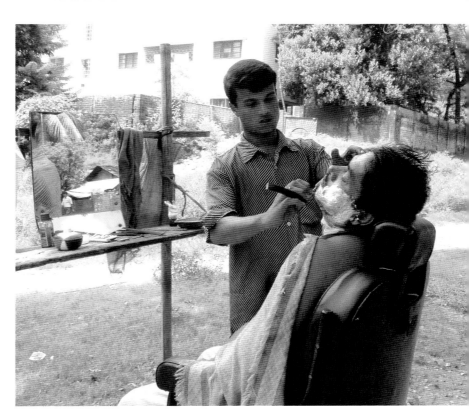

Barbers and Beauticians

The barber has set up shop in a field.
Women usually wear their hair long and rely on relatives for beauty needs.

Richer women avail themselves of the services of beauty parlors for eyebrow plucking, facials, and skin lightening.

Village
Vendors

Men do most of the shopping at the bazaars. The women stay home. However, vendors know that women like to buy things. So they carry their goods to them on their heads or on poles. Aluminum pots, plastic ware and produce are typical of the goods for sale.

Trash Trader

Earn a few taka by selling this man your trash. He will resell it with a little profit.

Garland Makers

Marigolds are strung together and used as traditional decoration for 'gaye holud'
(a ritual application of turmeric paste before weddings).

A bride in traditional dress.

A housewife is preparing food with a unique knife. Her foot holds the knife, freeing both hands to cut the fish which has been dipped in wood ash for a better grip. The knife is also used to slice vegetables or to cut meat.

Old cloth is transformed into quilts at home.

This young housewife will care for the one-day-old calf.

A refreshing bath.

Cow Milker

Milk Seller

The idea of owning a milk cow sounds romantic. The truth is that a cow is a lot of work. Grass must be cut — often far from home — for the cow's breakfast and dinner. When a calf is born, a small income comes from the fresh milk. The milkman makes the rounds of the neighborhood cows collecting milk to sell. At the end of the day he comes home with the empty pots.

Plowing in the Rain

It is pouring rain, but the farmer stays dry under his bamboo basket 'raincoat.'

Carpenters

Woodworkers work together using hand power instead of electricity to make furniture and cabinets.

Bamboo Workers

Bamboo is a versatile building material. Here, workers are cutting and weaving it into mats to build a traditional gazebo.

Firewood Gatherers

Sometimes it is difficult to believe that there is any firewood left in the country. Women and children carry firewood back to the village on their heads.

Wood Workers

Two men saw a fallen tree to sell for firewood while a woman collects twigs.
The men pull a log up an incline to cut up later.

Carnival Rides

The carnival ride made of wood and bamboo is popular at local fairs.

Balloon Salesman

*Evening is the most popular time to shop. This vendor stands in front of
a large shop. He knows that the shoppers may want to
buy a little something for their children.*

Rickshaws

Although trucks and buses seem to dominate the roads, it is the rickshaw that is the most popular form of transportation, especially in the smaller towns and villages.

A craftsman is painting a rickshaw.

A repairman has set up his tools by the side of the road waiting for customers. Rickshaws in need of repair surround another repairman.

Rickshaw Repair

Hotels

They are called 'hotels', but they are actually small cafes. These restaurants usually serve working and unemployed men. Some women buy 'take-away' items. Much of the food is fried, but some hotels have clay ovens, where 'naan ruti' is baked.

Snacks for Sale

Inexpensive ice cream is for sale from a pushcart. A man waits for customers to buy the rice cakes (pitha) from his small shop.

Livestock Market

Butchers buy cows at twice-weekly fairs. Once a year, families shop for cows, goats and even camels (brought from the Middle East), bring them home and sacrifice them for the Eid-ul-Azha Festival.

Sugar Cane

Sugar cane is cut in sections
and passed through a press
to make a refreshing drink.

Buffalo Cart

Manpower is used for most hauling work in the cities.
Outside the city, water buffaloes pull carts.

Pottery

Keep your Bangladeshi fresh flowers in a hand painted pottery vase.
Purchase an earthern ware bank for your taka coins from the pottery cart.

Flute Seller

A flute seller demonstrates a flute for customers at a fair.

Produce Hawker

This produce hawker is selling carrot snacks. Next week you might find him hawking bananas.

Honey Seller

Honeycombs are sold by the side of a village road.

Knife Sharpener

This man is ready to sharpen your knives. Could he be the same man who walked around my neighborhood when I was a little girl in Washington, DC?

Iftar Stall

Money for sale

The most important month of the Islamic calendar is the holy month of Ramadan. Muslims fast from sunrise to sunset, breaking their fast (Iftar) with traditional food.

The end of Ramadan is celebrated with new clothes and often presents for children in the form of taka, the currency of Bangladesh.

These men are selling crisp new taka bills.

Goldsmith

The artisan makes and repairs gold jewelry.

Political Activists

These women are marching to support their chosen political party.

The flag-seller knows that thousands of people will be on the street soon, on their way to a political rally.

Well Diggers

Clean water is in short supply. Many people have their own wells dug.

Roof Caster

Balancing a concrete mixture on his head, a workman climbs a bamboo scaffolding to help cast a new roof.

House Wreckers

Tearing down the old to make way for the new with pickaxes.

The Future Is ...

New buildings and new lifestyles are changing the traditional landscape of Bangladesh and replacing much of the traditional patterns of work. Celebrate the workers of Bangladesh!

The Play-Park

Children's Play Park at Bhatiary in Chittagong.

Royalties from the sale of this book will be used to support
a children's play park and club house in the village of Bhatiary.

Author with children at the play park.

Alpha Pictures